BOA
EDITIONS
LIMITED

Angels for the Burning

T0163960

Angels for the Burning

❖

POEMS BY
DAVID MURA

AMERICAN POETS CONTINUUM SERIES, NO. 89

BOA Editions, Ltd. ❖ *Rochester, NY* ❖ *2004*

Publications by BOA Editions, Ltd.—a not-for-profit corporation under
section 501 (c) (3) of the United States Internal Revenue Code—are made
possible with the assistance of grants from the Literature Program of the
New York State Council on the Arts; the Literature Program of the National
Endowment for the Arts; the Sonia Raiziss Giop Charitable Foundation; the
Lannan Foundation; the Mary S. Mulligan Charitable Trust; the County of
Monroe, NY; the Rochester Area Community Foundation; the Elizabeth F.
Cheney Foundation; the Ames-Amzalak Memorial Trust in memory of
Henry Ames, Semon Amzalak and Dan Amzalak; the CIRE Foundation,
as well as contributions from many individuals nationwide.

See Colophon on page 120 for special individual acknowledgments.

Cover Design: Daniel Wanglin
Cover Art: "Homage to Boat People" by Long Nguyen, courtesy of the artist
Interior Design and Composition: Richard Foerster

BOA Logo: Mirko

Library of Congress Cataloging-in-Publication Data

Mura, David.
 Angels for the burning / by David Mura. — 1st ed.
  p. cm. — (American poets continuum series ; v. 89)
 ISBN 1-929918-58-5 (pbk.paper)
 I. Title. II. Series.

PS3563.U68A84 2004
811'.54—dc22

2004018529

NATIONAL
ENDOWMENT
FOR THE ARTS

BOA Editions, Ltd.

A. Poulin, Jr., President & Founder (1938–1996)
250 North Goodman, Suite 306
Rochester, NY 14607
www.boaeditions.org

State of the Arts

NYSCA

for Susie, Samantha, Nikko, & Tomo

Contents

❧ IV ☙

❧ V ☙

Astronomy

I live amid a people not my own.
Yet on summer nights, Orion's belt
still hovers in its quadrant

just off the Dipper as
father said it always would.
At my second-story window

I stand with oaken creatures
stalking hundreds of feet
into the air, their leaves

whispering like my father—
*Connect the constellations like dots
star by star.* Once I knew the names

and places of all the planets,
galaxies, nebulae, and dwarfs,
recited them before company

in the living room, then slurped my
glass of RC with Pepperidge Farm
Goldfish and trudged off to bed.

Tonight the house is hushed
with scents of lilacs and leaves
and their shadows sway

through the room where my sons
entreat me to tell of the time
I hid beneath my bed

and no one, grandpa nor grandma,
could find their wayward son.
The room is dark, the moon

floats on the floor. I spy the stars
over the houses and murmuring
a prayer with my boys, wonder

how it is I lost Arcturus,
Orion, and even the Dipper,
all those galaxies and stars

spinning inside them,
father, mother, wayward son—
And how later and later

and later I came to be found.

Relocations

for Grandfather Uyemura

People married by pictures then;
when they lied, the bride stepped
from the ship and found a dwarf,
nose gnarled as a ginger root.

He was so handsome, he came
in person, held her as America rose
and fell ahead. Gulls shrieked;
on the dock, the pale ghosts gathered.

*

He bought a greenhouse on a field
hand's wages, and with Cuban cigar
jammed in his jaw, watched his
orchids like petulant courtesans.

Nights, the eucalyptus swayed,
his eyes gleamed with his Packard's
chrome beneath the moon. He slapped his
thighs, rubbed the dirt from his hands,

prayed for dice clicking sevens.
By dawn he was whistling home.
He stumbled in roses,
said hello to the thorns.

*

When they shipped them like cattle
to the camps, he sat in the mess hall
and creased a napkin like the nine-ply
folds of heaven; out of his hands

flew a slim, white crane. His wife
shook her head, smiled, forgot barbed
wire, guards. At a mule-pulled plow
he wiped his baseball cap across

his brow, looked past the wires to
the prairie where the west begins. Tipping
his cap to the corporal in the tower,
he muttered "Bakka," picked up the reins.

*

He named his son Katsuji, prince
of birds. After the war it was Tom,
such a strange name, like someone
beating a drum, hollow, a hard echo.

He laughed at the boy's starving
Jesus, nails piercing the little bones
of the hands and feet, told him
the Buddha always ate well.

When she died, he returned to Tokyo.
Still attached to his body, limbs
folded on a chair, he spent
his evenings composing haiku—

> *Bonsai tree*
> *like me you are useless*
> *and a little sad.*

Tatsue's Prophecies

I am the daughter of a fisherman
who trolled the pebbled shore off Shingu's sea,
who mended his nets season after season
and grappled up fish as I grappled dreams:

As a girl I gazed hours before that horizon,
and even then was sailing away,
so that when mother later looked there
was only empty air the rest of her days.

Long ago, in Nippon, they told how travelers,
at the fork of their forest journeys,
were netted at night by witches or spirits:
Who scries the future must haunt the living.

Once I dreamt my husband with his temple
strapped in bandages, seeping with blood.
Nonsense, he said, strutting out for his day.
Came back as I dreamed, bloody and bowed.

Later I foresaw air filled with tails of fire,
fire heaped like sun after sun on a city;
and in one house my sleeping older sister:
I could not wake her, spirit without pity.

We lived then by swamps in sweltering heat,
penned in like demons and kept from wandering;
so often my dreams severed my sanity
and brought me prophecy but never peace.

Now I wake dawns to tend my garden
and fill my hours as my children flee
into America with their American names,
though I gave birth to them in Japanese.

Last night I dreamed a gray gray woman
lifting daikon, *chizo*, chrysanthemum:
But she could find no children to cook for,
nor even he who once asked for my future

as a girl in Shingu, gazing from that shore.

No Epic Song

1. *Strawberry Fields*

Trace these acres pressed by shovels and spades.
By crows, worms, and drought. Darkness

like a tide sliding in. The woman calls
evening at the field's edge. A baby

bawls back in the cabin. *Gohan*
cools on a wooden table.

The horizon's opulent, obedient as the sun
which rises each day without calling

or prodding; not
like the *biwa* player working this earth

and dreaming *hana fuda*
fetching alien

coins. A sip of *sake*.
A drunk walk home. Thus will moonlight

limn him to the outer edges of this land
and a consciousness brimming

with haiku
so unlike anything he sees—

snow flakes fall to the sea
where do they go

where do they go

2. Ojii-san Interned

A man ambles ten paces from barbed-wire fences—
Possessing no livelihood nor country nor dissent,

hovers with others nights by a burning oil drum,
warms his hands and moans to the *biwa*'s drone:

Prince Atsumori and clan in the blood thrashed tide.
Tales of epic loss. Glorious deaths. Beautiful lies.

Sparks shower up in his face
which glows by the fire as a poor man must

and the notes quaver as the strings twang
almost a delta blues, quavering quarter tones.

This to me is the ancient world.
This and thorns of lost strawberry fields.

And why is it nothing after bears this trace—
his death his freedom the redress too late

much less his son's promotions
as insurance executive

or the birth of a first grandson
who writes this poem?

3. *Minidoka*

Once a fence post sank here in its ground,
dug in by spades and shovels and boredom.
Along with other posts, barbed wire, and guards,
it hid three thousand in a place called Minidoka.

A day of infamy said Roosevelt to Congress.
Dirty Japs imprinted headlines of Hearst.
My god they're coming said mothers and fathers on the coast.
My god they're here said passers-by on the streets.

I don't recall said mother in Morton Grove.
I played baseball there said father in his Buick.
(So many songs of protest. Ours isn't one.
It's smaller and more lost. Resolutely silent.)

I walk among remnants of boards and wires,
indentations in earth where once they slept.
A spoon, a wire figurine. *Hashi.* A doll's limb.
Wind whips through the prairie. The afternoon darkens.

Town full of no one, not even shadows of fences.
A site in the desert no one breathes.
And who are the invaders and who the prisoners.
And who stands guard here. Or witness. Or thief.

4. *Xmas in Las Vegas*

Down the valley casinos shout out their lights.
A spire like a space station towers over all.
Guests from Taiwan, Hong Kong, Singapore,
now welcomed with Japanese, gamblers all.

It's no more a white country. Or so I tell father.
Who knows better than me what here succeeds.
Blue Shield Vice President. Moderate Republican.
His back window opens to the par five twelfth.

What have I to say to that? Or mother's white
carpets where grandchildren unwrap and unwrap.
It seems there's no end, a cornucopia of days.
Why stand in the shadows. In the cold past.

No. Vegas is a crapshoot. Play it as it lays.

Bruyères (1944)

Here is the village, here the steeple, here
the fields where cows munch lazily and bray.
Here by wildflowers and tall wheat, a huge stone
bursts to white bits at a sniper's ricochet.

Someone's hiding behind the stone. A Nisei
with my uncle's eyes, a grape farmer's son.
All morning he's threaded through woods and fields,
his Buddhahead platoon prying out Germans.

The sniper's by the barn, the pen of pigs,
a farmhouse where a frightened family
fled hours ago. Stiffened behind the stone,
the soldier sees it must be made quickly,

the choice of breaking for the barn or breaking
down here, weeping and weakening the line.
Two crows cackle overhead, and a cow
lows by the willows, lapping at the stream.

A bullet rips a chunk. The man recoils,
memories spill forth against oblivion:
Okaa-san stares out the door at Heart Mountain;
the peaks and towers, fences the far horizon.

Or how he hated his old man muttering
hayaku, long into that harvesting dark.
How some vines are saved from the shears,
others clipped for the good bark to flourish.

He hears Tak cry out, spies a green flak jacket
flat on the field, a rough brushstroke
that marks the canvas, and then the bark
of his sergeant, *Let's go, Izumi, let's go.*

And so he leaps, no longer stone.

Internment Camp Psychology

circa 1945

Just after his release Mas took a psychological test.

Three questions he never forgot: Do you think

people are out to get you? Do you feel you are

being followed? When you see a crowd of strangers

walking toward you, do you try to avoid them?

To all three he answered yes.

And knew he sounded insane.

Years Later

The children in bed, the two of us out back
drift to the flicker of birds—or is it bat wings?—
squirrels, freeway traffic, crickets ticking the night.

A bare bulb shimmers above us, so faint
I scarcely scan the pages. (And yet I read on.
Some desires are impossible to extinguish.)

In my father's yearbook, dusty from the attic,
a young man, torso bare, ribs rippled, struts
shirtless by the flagpole at the center of camp.

Befitting the "best body" in Denson High, '44,
did he love his own dark-skinned beauty,
as he loved my mother these many years?

I think of Pearl and Roosevelt's orders,
the spies we never were, days in those swamps,
a lost nursery and greenhouse he never mentioned.

Or how, beneath the alley stairs, a boy
heard his father call through late afternoon light
a name from the Bible, translated Beloved,

and could not tell a soul why he was hiding,
whether from the bully Michael Ogata
or something more secret he could not name.

Years later, I sit behind a house so immense,
it hardly seems mine, though the children
inside have filtered through my blood

scrapes on their knees, cries when they waken
in the dark, spirited by fear, as they wander
to my arms, the chance night needs to hold us all.

It's a strange, buoyant business we exchange.
I know this woman whose blessings are enormous,
like the cedars of Lebanon, more than I can grasp.

I see how a wave of talking shored between us
waters we navigated so many years.
I taste salt on my tongue, the promise of summer,

look up and unleash these errant prayers. A siren
sings from the highway, a dog howls next door.
I know I've waited all my life to sit like this.

First Generation Angels

They lived behind the firehouse and Little Saigon Auto.
In spring he sat on the porch while his mother,
the manicurist at Khan's salon, clipped his hair.
Smells of lilac, exhaust. A siren sucking up the distance.
A black corona drops to his shoulders. An impatient sigh.

How soon he vanished from her. Like his father staring
from the couch at the color TV, his black veteran's cap
from the surplus store sliding a mask over his eyes.
Five sisters, three brothers. Smells of *pho* and coriander.
While he's gone to fry stacks of tortillas at Little Tijuana's.

With lean bad ass cheeks. Hair pomaded back. A thin mustache.
You know then he's written poems decrying *Miss Saigon*.
His life as Nuprin, a little yellow pill for your pains.
His uncle dead years ago in a paddy. VC bullet in his brow.
He and his poems will read next week at Patrick's Cabaret.

But if you look from your salsa and he's not in the kitchen?
You fear he's sitting in a room with the social worker,
the clock above ticking, the lawyer not yet arrived, and he
recording his story, muttering I've outlived all your stories,
man. Eyes like a panther. A caged bird. A jaded small boy.

Back in the apartment his mother conjures with the shaman,
rocks to and fro for the spirits, so far from Laos hills,
herbal hallucinogens that once brought them forth.
Hot blood wrung from a rooster's neck. Ancestral prayers.
Her head wrapped in a black cloth, her eyes dry weeping.

Then you know he's not Vietnamese. That Mai was with him.
That she was the one shouting, *Shoot him, shoot the motherfucker.*
And the other girl screaming. He staring at the dark pool.
Man, I didn't know you could bleed that much. . . . How'd they find us?
The words won't translate. Like years ago, winter at the window—

He's looking down University, his head echoing with
his father's nightmares, his mother's weeping. He marks
the tire tracks, a cop car sluicing past. Then it's nothing
but snow and snow and snow, and each flake a small angel
sprouting wings in the dark, spiraling down upon us all.

The Young Asian Women

The young Asian women are shaving their heads,
piercing eyelids and ears. They stare holes
in curators, shop clerks and geisha chasers,
bubble gum snapping like caps in their jaws.
Their names? Juliana, Vong, Lee, and Lily.
Could be Mina from the outskirts of Tokyo
but more likely she's Nkauj'lis of the famous
or infamous Lyfongs (depending on your clan
and your anti-Communist persuasions).
Check out that siren named Sonia, too in love
with her looks, a nasty curl of Seoul
in her smile. Or if her name is Hoa,
she's tough as her mother, bad girl, bitch,
it doesn't matter, she'll survive like nettles,
flower in what ditch she finds herself, with
or without a man, or her lesbian lover who left
for Alaska, the smell of bear shit on the trail.
With her Taiwanese aunt, digs tales of Toisan
ladies, dragons and the water marsh where bandit
ghosts steal years with a kiss, talking tongues
down your throat to your belly, slipping
a demon seed inside you to grow. Oh, they're
like that, these young women, their art alive
like Thai hot sauce on your tongue, hurtling hurt
with a half pint gleaming on the night stand.
They know how mysteriously the body is written,
how thundering colors of Benetton befit
statistics on garment workers in the Third
and First Worlds. They know *Woman Warrior*,
bell hooks, how the moon waxes red like
the sheets where they write out scripts, stories,
and poems, unwrapping their dreams before
you, a palm of paint, pearls, I-Ching stones.
With boots black and buckled, their jeans frayed,

lips bruised purple or incandescent red,
their bodies at the dance club cut into hip-hop.
Their voices are hoarse after nights on the floor,
their faces smeared with sweat. Their cheeks aglow.
They scare the pants off the young men they know.

Words on My Tongue

I am eight, sitting in a circle with our teacher.
I am to read out loud. Though I know these words
—*ball, the, I, throw, boy, girl*—they lodge
in my throat, dry as cotton balls, a cough that won't leave.
My teacher wears a look of concern or impatience,
it doesn't matter. My classmates giggle or shift
in boredom, it doesn't matter. The words
lie like ammunition. I will not fire them.
The minutes pass, the day is long. Finally,
the teacher asks the next student to read on.

Deep at night, that first winter,
I lay in the cupola
of my sheets and rubbed
my hands together, half
in prayer, half
like two sticks, praying for fire.
Like those who took us in
as sponsors on Sunday,
I was asking for the Holy Spirit
to enter me, to speak in tongues of flame.

We were Chinese, from Sadec, just outside Saigon.
There the river flooded through the delta,
a miracle of mud and substances abounding
in the current—crates, chairs, water buffalo, branches,
and sometimes bodies, the drowned
ones, eyes turned toward some other world.
My brother almost drowned there once.
My mother slapped me for taking him down.
That sting still rings in my ear like a gong.

I knew I spoke with this accent.
It was visible as a hump
or the limp my sister walks with,

the metal braces that reverberate her steps.
The noise that emptied from my mouth
contained a color I could not eradicate,
a grating singsong
like horsehair of a violin, a Chinese violin,
and even as I opened my mouth
I could see, in the eyes of a listener,
if they were white, spreading in every direction
across their face, a judgment
as inevitable as at evening
comes the descending night.

Uncomely noise, ugly noise, ching-chong
Chinamen noise, cavity ridden
and sounding of brown gums, yellowed teeth,
contorted lips struggling like some ape to speak,
and unlike the splinter
father drew with delicacy from my palm,
removing a pain I'd lived with all day,
down the streets of the city, the graffiti and traffic,
there was nothing he could do,
nor my mother. The words sat
on my tongue, like the questions
that sat inside my ear—*What did you say? What did he say?*

Still,
even then, I was moving away,
coming to the time
when I would stand with father, mother,
before my teacher
and translate to them
both the praise, which I embellished,
and the checks, which I altered, fights
on the asphalt schoolyard of broken glass
and a rumbling in my stomach
that spoke incessantly of fear.
Deep in the magical jungle,
in some country we traveled

to, my parents were wandering,
and I had to lead them, word by word,
in the grocer's, before the lawyer, my teacher,
to meaning, sweet land of comprehension
rising like an island from the chaos of oceans
back in the beginning when God made the word and the world.

You children, you who take your foreign parents
into these unfamiliar streets
know this trembling, this fear;
and even though you speak *for* them,
you cannot speak your fear.

And yet
the minutes pass, the day is long,
and the smirk in their smiles, the sliver on your tongue,
it all must vanish like the words you spoke
as a child:

Boy, ball, throw, me. . . .

Father Blues for Jon Jang

Way back in the fifties
      when Chinaman was a chink
            and chance a Chinaman's dance,

and Charlie Chan still yellowed
      his wizened fat face in a cinema
            of blue-eyed blonds;

with white boys blowing blues,
      as angel-headed hipsters
            coked and toked their dreams

on the road, in Beat Bay cafés;
      back when Chinatown
            danced *Flower Drum Song*—

Well, once in that glorious decade,
      my father's rising, Ph.D.
            in chemistry, crashing

glass ceilings of Fluor Corporation
      with brains and acumen
            and easygoing laugh,

and like any white blue-blooded American
      screening *Leave It To Beaver*, *Donna
            Reed*, and *Father Knows Best*,

father had to score a house,
      and no one could call him
            Hey Boy, Hop Sing,

or Peter the cranky *Bachelor Father* houseboy,
            forget those Stepin Fetchit
                        chinky figures of fun, Baba

got a house jones, come hell or highwater,
            so he banked bids on house after
                        house all across this city,

and after every bid they told him
            politely—or impolitely, it didn't really matter—Solly!
            Charlie Chinaman,

you don't stand a chance!
            Even if your offer bounces higher than the price,
                        even if you send the price soaring

like the homers of the Say Hey
            Kid blasting over the fence,
                        no way, wing-wong, NO WAY!

—But never a man to trip "No," Baba
            steered a white friend to bid on this house, higher
                        than the asking,

and his proxy copped the house,
            taking commission on the side,
                        and now we're living high on the hog

on a hill over Chinatown and the Bay,
            and father queued for Vice President, better salaries,
                        bigger cars, the whole shebang . . .

And then. And then: SLAM—HEADLINE:
            June 29, 1956, *New York Times*:
                        126 Die in Plane Crash

down the Grand Canyon, the
            decade's largest disaster, larger
                        than any other for me

with my father aboard, Baba's
       remains mangled beyond
              recognition in the crumpling

crush of metal, pyres of high octane
       flames. And Woo's Funeral Parlor
          serviced what was left,

and inside Woo's roaring oven,
       a small stellar blast
          seared my father

down to a vase of ash, slipped
       inside a lacquered wooden box,
             and my mother, three months

pregnant, hauled it in
       to be interred in the Glendale Cemetery,
             her other arm tugging along, barely

two, a toddler teetering from the Chevy,
       half conscious
          something was now amiss, amid

rolling lawns and slabs of stone
       and the office where my mother stood, waiting
          to tomb what was left

of father in a vault,
       and I don't know why, don't
          savvy, my mother

crying, screaming, yanking
       me out of that office, cursing in Chinese
          the white man behind the desk,

and only years later do I catch my father
       couldn't be buried there once
          they made my mother, once

they scried her eyes, her skin, her
    lithe dark figure, her eyes, her skin
        in the boy beside her,

and the moral charts, I suppose,
    what I've carted to this day—
        "It don't matter if you're flamed

down to ash, just primal dust,
    you still a Chinaman, you might as well
        blow your life, your music that way

—Oh Chinaman Chinaman Chinaman blues . . ."

The Angel of Phillips Park

Two crows in the alley garbage, shrieking
and scuffling at a leg bone or stale egg sandwich,
and the night, impatient, takes them down,
their raucous throats and wing flurry now silent.

Night of the first lilacs. Just after a strong spring rain.
Wiping out for a few hours the dealers at the corner,
fists in their baggy pants, Nikes sliding the walk,
black hoods or knit caps, bleary eyes catching it all.

In the park on Franklin, outside the Four Winds School,
the last kid, on the scholarship of his mind, pops
the air with arcs, trey after trey, counting the final
seconds of his game, and the crowd roars in his ears

like the ocean he's never seen, and just as he hits
the top of the key, the first shot steels through
the sternum, one then his shooting hand, so quick
pulling the trigger, and it flows from the porous spot

draining his belly like a black hole in the heavens,
and on this court where he always won and gave it all,
his body topples in a puddle so epic and slow in its fall,
some bit of his brain's still hot, *Made it, nothing but net.*

Silence now, stepping through wet grass. Held in check
till the flashing lights and the tires of the city's finest
screech to the tennis courts. The static on the radio
mikes 10–4 breaking up. The crows start at it again.

And no one sees one rising higher and higher on wings
of blackness and prayer, a jam so devastating
and powerful, redeeming all the light in this universe
and giving it back as a crow, a night, a boy, a star.

Island Angel

On Pacita Abad's "How Mali Lost Her Accent"

Father, where is the sea? The surf of my heart?
The girls with their twirling skirts of memory,
Who go down to the waves, soaking their garments.
Whose hearts were white. Whose skin was dark.

(Now I live where these colors are reversed.)
The swells were so blue there. And the nights.
Yes, we there sometimes hated our blackness.
But in secret, in secret we loved it even more.

You tell me our life here is new. And I believe you.
It's just: I believe them too. Their loud loud voices.
On the streets. In my class. On the chalkboards.
Numbers in my notebook. The flag above my desk.

Inside my chest I still hold corridors of sunlight.
Villages where palms and pomegranates and linen blow.
Streets where people simply walk, day by day, into their lives.
The dust beneath their soles. The rain. The mud.

Father, I know I'll forget all this.
I'll be different then. I will.
No longer your angel.
No longer yours.

Fong

"The gun? Shit. Everyone's got a gun.
I go down to the park, find someone,
buy a Tech, a Gloch. A twenty-two for two Jacksons,
less than four CDs. Everyone's got one.

Say some dude eyeballs me, gets in my face.
I'm gonna get in his, I'm gonna say,
Whachu want asshole. But I don't got a drive-by.
He does. I'm fucked. Can't say a thing, can I?

Mai? I guess she's my girl. We just hang together.
She's wicked, Mai, she got this edge on her.
I think, if she'd had the gun, not me. . . .
She kept on yellin', *pop him, pop the motherfucker.*

Man, there was a lot of blood. Who knew
he could bleed that much? Like a swimming pool.
Maybe I saw all that blood I got a little scared,
the girls was screamin' and we all scattered. . . .

I didn't think they'd find us. How'd they find us?
They came right up to our apartment steps.
My mom was cryin', she didn't get it.
Just like on TV. Yellin' and screamin' and shit.

Why'd we rob the store? Fuck, who knows?
Buy some beer, cigarettes, maybe a boombox.
It don't matter. So they haul me in here.
I'm a juvy, right? Worst I get is five years.

Back in Laos, my uncles, they all got pieces.
Jumped the jungle at night, killed for the CIA.
Here ain't no warriors, ain't no war.
There's just us kids. Just us gangsters."

In the Video Store at Chicago & Lake

From that darkness of my wallet, a moistness
wafted out, half the sweat of my own fat body,
half the bills fingered by stranger after stranger,

and as the video clerk shuffled back to the stacks
for *Black Orpheus*, I prepared to pay. Then sensed
beside me a smile—One gold tooth, a bicuspid missing.

Grizzled white whiskers hissing some soft sibilant.
Then *Hey brother,* as if I were one of his tribe.
When I turned full face to his *You got a dollar?*

I mumbled so inaudibly even I couldn't tell
what I was saying. I glanced down in my wallet.
His cracked lips whispered again, *Come on brother,*

not bothering with *Cup of coffee. . . . something to eat.*
And *Shit,* he didn't say. Nor, *Fuck man, it's just a dollar.*
(Still I couldn't help but think: One dollar leads to another.)

Moments passed. I fingered up the thin worn bill.
He laughed, *That's what we call taking care,*
it all comes back, brother, it all comes back.

Maybe someday you'll need a dollar and I'll help you,
that's the way we do things back where I come from.
And I asked where's that, and he, *Chattanooga,*

and I echoed, *Chattanooga,* as if another world.
Then the clerk came back and before he noticed,
the old black man in the soiled blue baseball jacket

slipped out as easily as he'd slipped in.

Black Angel: Latasha Harlins

The angel walked into the corner store
and opened the back cooler
and whether the orange juice she placed
in her back pack said convenience
or shoplift, we'll never know. All
we know is her mother one night
danced this party to Earth, Wind & Fire
and the air smelled of eucalyptus,
cigarettes, smog, liquor, and perfume,
black bodies awash with each other
and when the night was over, a knife
like an exclamation point stood
upright from her chest, and the partyers
vanished into the dawn like spirits
or ordinary black folk who must do
what they do. And her daughter? All
we know is she'd found herself
having left her grandmother's house
and on her way to school, face
to face with a harpy or a human
mask of fear, a Korean or mother
to someone she'd never know,
but they knew each other, customer
and owner, arguing over whether
she'd paid for it all. Then the owner
swung a stool on the counter, snapped
her young black hand, strewing change
toward the register, and the girl
smacked that mask, grabbed for the stool,
and like a wishbone between them
they pulled it apart, like a game
between two children tugging at war
and no thought of the moment
coming up in the handgun
like a viper risen from behind

the counter, a will all its own,
striking for her life, once, twice,
three, four times, and though she,
the owner, has seen it all
on the videotape of the monitor,
she cannot recall how the girl
turned her back to her and revealed
two tiny wings there, fluttering
with the gift of forgiveness or flight.

❖ **III** ❖

Minneapolis Public

There are 150 first languages in our schools
and so many aliens even E.T. would go unnoticed,
though if your tongue moved one way in the land of your birth
it must move another now, awkward at first.

There are blacks here who've never been to Africa;
Africans who've never heard a Baptist prayer,
much less the solemn dirges of Lutherans
or how the artist formerly known is some sort of Prince.

In the anthology of American Buddhist poetry
you will find not one face of a Tibetan
but they are here with girls and boys named Tenzin
and one, my son's good friend, throws a hard mean spiral.

Esmir is not the name of a girl but a Bosnian
boy who crouches at a table and glues a lamp together
and later with my other son conspires on a book—"A Touch
of Rabies"—a heartbreaking tale of good dogs gone bad.

(Why tell a soul of the sieges that brought him here
or stories of the Dali Lama and the temples destroyed
or troops of the warlords in the streets of Somalia,
the borders dividing death from safety if not evil and good?)

Say you're Egyptian or Haitian: Here you're singular,
not part of a Big Apple ghetto. If you're Chinese,
most likely you're adopted, or else your parents study
engineering at the U. And have I mentioned the Mexicans?

In *West Side Story* the rumble starts with Puerto Ricans
and working-class whites in a high-school gym;
this year Maria's still Natalie Wood white to Jamaica's
half-black Anita, and the Jets sport blacks, one Tibetan,

and my *happa* daughter who still doesn't question
such casting, or why *Bye Bye Birdie* last year
just might not be the choice of half the school
for a song and dance they could take on as their own.

Still at the spring school dance J.Lo and Ja Rule
set the awkward bump and grind of junior high girls
and the boys watch on the sidelines as boys that age do,
whether Bosnian, black, white, Somali, Tibetan.

I'm told we live in the Land of Great Lake Wobegon
where all the women are strong, the men good-looking,
and the children above average—and, I always add,
everyone's white. Hey, Tenzin, Nabil, go tell Garrison:

Not now. Not quite.

Legend

An only daughter is a needle in the heart
was how, in one legend, a poet put it.
Thus the legends of the father at the start of war
say I must stand on a rocky shore
and beg the gods for winds to cross the waters
and battle and destroy the city Troy.
And the gods shout back: Sacrifice your daughter.
Or else, in the tale of seven samurai swords,
I first hide you from brigands
and then from the warriors
who would save us for daily rations of rice.
And what these legends tell us is
the desires of fathers are foolish
with fear of their enemies and hatred in their hearts.
And fear too of how his daughter will part
her legs and never be seen again
for this is what happens
when men write the legends.
Of course there is no father in these tales
who descends down the corridors of hell
and crosses those foul and mysterious waters
to retrieve from the underworld his only daughter
and finds the courage to return her each year
before the leaves may bud and the earth flower.
Today I wandered with you
through the aisles of Abercrombie & Fitch
where all beaming models are ruddy and blond
and no dark face mars their endless summer.
And I want to tell you they are there
to make themselves rich
and not because they are foolish and fond
and love the way your black
hair shimmers down your lanky brown back.
But I know you will not listen if I tell you.

I am the father, my words could destroy you.
Or bar you from the one blushing samurai
who gathers flowers on the hill
and though he desires to know what it is to kill,
what he desires most is beyond her father
as she opens for him on a slope of bright flowers
this summer afternoon with no thought of death
or how someone must descend in cold autumn showers
and answer to darkness and darker desires.

Suite for Miss Saigon

for my daughter

1. *Prologue: Taking Samantha to the Protest*

We're weaving through hard traffic this evening,
late for the plush new Ordway Theater,
the sky behind us sheets of palomino.

This is your second *Saigon* protest.
(Like Dracula, it keeps coming back.)
Why play this game again? a part of me asks.

This morning you read an essay I've written.
You ask why, as a boy worshipping Paladin
striding the hotel stairs, hipped with six-guns,

I never recalled the messenger hollering,
paper in fist, pig-tail flapping from out
his black beanie, "Teragram for Mr. Paradin!"

I try to explain. You nod, then say,
"I think whites don't like to talk about race."
I look to your eyes, your sun-darkened face:

Like Yeats' dancer, a blossoming bole
quickly unfolding, how soon your selves vanish.
Where is that girl in the pink pinafore,

replaced by one who sliced her Barbies in parts,
to be glued and stacked in installation art
protesting such simpering plastic ways?

Replaced by this tween in lime green, perusing
teen magazines, posting her wall with ads
for Skechers, *Felicity*, stars from WB.

Years ago, you asked why certain friends vanished,
those you recall, if at all, as strangers in photos,
vague figures in our kitchen or yard, laughing

as you waddled by or played your games.
Dear, here's how it happened. Why is more difficult to say.

*

Back in the days of my first performance art,
blasting Warner Oland as Charlie Chan,
Keye Luke the bumbling—"Gee, Pop!"—No. 1 son;

flush with that fevered yellow-eyed protest,
recanting years when white friends proffered,
"I think of you, David, just like a white person,"

I'm arguing with two close white friends
on the Broadway production of *Miss Saigon*:
Paula, a painter, and Mark, a poet, listen

as I rail on the white Brit thespian
donning Eurasian. (Not to mention her
Butterfly seppuku for the pure white john.)

As my voice rises to their questions,
you push a plastic pram, brimming puppies,
kittens, and bears, oblivious to tensions

stalking the room. You beg me to let you
finger-paint again. I tell you no,
turn on the TV, and my friends resume:

"Isn't colorblind casting what we're striving for?
"Isn't art entering other people's skin? . . .
"—But David, reverse discrimination isn't the answer!

*

"At the head of our alley appeared a large gang of toughs screaming, 'Americans go home! America go to hell! Go home!' And in the lurid light of their flickering torches these fanatical faces looked exactly like the cartoons of the Japanese barbarians we had kept posted in our ready rooms during the war. I remember one horrible face rushing at me. Distorted, evil, brutal, inhuman . . . The last thing I saw was a Japanese face—not the evil masks, but Hanaogi's oval and yellow beauty."
—*James Michener,* Sayonara

*

Last week I opened this spam in my mailbox:
*Japanese Girls are HOT! "THE BEST" in Japanese/
Asian porn sites   Just one look at this sweet hot
young Japanese on the front scolding her teddy . . .*

Within a future I can't quite change, some man
comes on to you in class, a street, or bar,
libido hot-wired with all these screenings
he denies, though not his desires;

and says how pleased, how absolved,
how freely he's commingled with the other,
so unencumbered by impediments of skin,
much less lost colonies and wars—

Will you recall, as he will not, *Miss Saigon?*

*

"Just what is it those people are protesting? . . .
Across the street, over there in the park."
A bell rings in the lobby for the opening.
The audience ambles in, the theater goes dark.

As the music kicks up, the libretto soars
with a coy twist on geishas from Puccini:
An innocent GI falls in love with a whore.
Her Eurasian pimp loves the loot she brings.

And by the time the Oriental girl sprawls
on stage, so eager to pass from this world,
as terror and pity, shivers and sobs descend
on rows of middle-aged middle-class women,

I'm sure they've long ago forgotten
the pony-tailed father and Eurasian daughter
who shouted from the park at startled patrons
and raised crude placards in inscrutable anger.

2. *The Tribe, The Dream*

"... in a series of telephone calls, I told Paula and Mark I not only felt that their views were wrong about *Miss Saigon* but that they were racially based. In the emotionally charged conversations, I don't think I used the word 'racist' but I know they both objected to my lumping them together with other whites. Paula said I was stereotyping them, that she wasn't like other whites. She told me of her friendships with a few blacks when she lived back East, of the history of her mother's involvement in supporting civil rights. 'It's not like I don't know what discrimination is,' she said. 'Women get discriminated against, so do artists.' Her tone moved back and forth between self-righteousness and resentment to distress and tears about losing our friendship.

Mark talked about his shame of being a WASP. 'Do you know that I don't have a single male friend who is a WASP?' he said. I decided not to point out that within the context of color, the difference between a WASP male and, say, an Irish Catholic, isn't much of a difference. And I also didn't remark that he had no friends of color, other than myself. I suppose I felt such remarks would hurt him too much. I also didn't feel it was safe to say them. . . ."

*

Knowing your bright and contrary ways, the thrusts and parries you practice with your mother and me,

should I tell you there are costs?

Later when I wrote about all this in *Mother Jones* —the arguments over *Miss Saigon,* the breakup—

here's how other mutual white friends answered in letters, in person, or in gossip:

"Have you become a racial separatist?"

"Can't you have white friends any longer?"

"The reward for the destruction of community is power."

"You violated Mark's privacy."

"You can write about your family like that. Not your friends."

"I don't want a guru on race."

"Don't you think it was all just personality?"

"I don't understand. Why can't you still be friends?"

"Is he going to leave Susie?"

"You can't hire him. . . . He dresses too well to be a minority."

"We're reducing the size of our editorial board."

"......" "......" "....."

*

In my dream one night, a black poet read
so softly her sequence on Rosa Parks,
and afterwards, in the cavernous cathedral,

the mainly white audience—this was St. Paul—
applauded longer than usual. Later
mingling, I joked with her white husband

about letters of protest he first, myself
following, had written against the Jim Crow
Chancellors of the American Academy.

Slowly the audience thinned out, the husband
and myself remaining. Then off to the side,
in a circle, I suddenly saw the friend I'd lost,

two other former writer friends, their husbands,
and I felt my unease gnarling within,
a knot I knew I should finally untie,

only I couldn't, I just couldn't. Then
the poet's husband and I moved up their aisle
to his wife waiting in the back,

and I thought, yes, it's not so difficult,
I could just say hello. Only as we drew closer,
my friends, my former friends, already

ambled in a loose and laughing cluster
up the aisle to the exit, their backs to me.
It didn't matter then what I did, or whether

it was just chance, casual and unplanned,
or even a pointed ritual shunning. . . .

—Daughter, I lied. This was no dream.

*

Today I mentioned the young Vietnamese poet
who told me no white boy could ever cruise
into his house, his daughter hand in hand:
"Hah," you spat, "I'd bring one home just to spite you!"

I cannot protect you from your growing body;
desires which draw us so far from ourselves.
You buy a ticket, you enter the lobby.
Await the play which tells how you'll fall.

Dear, once a boy despised the face in the glass
and found a fury there to feed his lust.
How could his skin reflect a glint of beauty?
I look at you now: It's there before me.

And if it is, a poet once proclaimed,
an invitation to a voyage,
forgive me if I do not always know
where you are traveling or when to let go.

Two Imperialist Ditties

1. *A Little Song from Kipling*

There was a little brown brother.
There was a little brown sister.
The brother called us master.
The sister called us mister.

And yes their country was warm
And easy like a woman;
We sampled each and all her charms
Until she turned a demon.

Oh damn the East and all its lies,
Oh damn those ugly heathens;
Damn their beauty and their spies,
And take me back to heaven.

2. Caliban's Curse

You taught me language; and my profit on't
Is, I know how to curse. . . .
———The Tempest

Oh Mr. Motto Fu Manchu
Kung Fu ninja chopping you
Charlie Chan
chink and jap man

houseboy gardener laundry coolie
Miss Saigon's chop-chop suey
this is how our balls were banned
this is where they played our parts

fuck their yellow minstrel farce
fuck them in their white white hearts
fuck them till they fall apart
weeping for their white white art

Darker Desires

Oh back in the glorious age of colonization,
                as the first boats spilled
                                their dark African cargo
to Caribbean isles;

or sweaty Conquistadors
                told some terrifying
                                (terrified?) Aztec beauty
to love him long time, some

began to worry
                how the permanence of racial lines
                                could be reconciled
with the fertility

of interracial fucking:
                The master and native
                                so rudely rutting
in bordello, jungle, slave quarters.

This
                has nothing to do,
                                say, with love poetry,
though lovers and lunatics do

share a certain imagination. (Sigh.)

                        *

At fourteen our daughter
sunbathes in her bikini
in the dunes at the Cape,

assimilated to a bad pop song
in the eyes of teenage boys
playing volleyball up the ridge.

She does not see me staring at her, hair
flaring in black flames, as she
romps into seething foam, swirling

at her dark roan thighs,
and dives under
and waves wash over her slipping

from my sigh, just the surge
of their crashing
and the riptide that might pull her out.

I made a promise never to write about her.
I made a promise never to grow old.
I made a promise to be faithful to her mother.

Desire must be hot, promises cold.

*

Study the shadows and creases of the rinds—
Olive, aubergine; pepper, papaya, and dusky melon.

How the fruits of the earth opened before us.
How their juices spilled from our lips.

Donned riding boots, pith helmets, whips.
Playing polo in the darkest of continents.

Pitching our tents. Arms draped
over girls in sarongs. Wild birds squawking above.

A man enters by parting the flaps.
Vines like snakes slither from the trees.

*

In yellow rhapsody and this blue millennium
before the ghosts of my ancestors

what of my daughter
who clips no photos of Asian guys

to her walls where Angels Cameron, Drew, and Lucy Liu,
toss long locks in the winds of desire

which drives the black girls mad
though no one notices but in hip-hop,

Missy Elliott strutting "boys, boys. . . .
black white Puerto Rican Chinese boys"

and ching-chong samples a chorus
wound backwards so no one deciphers?

*

*"It may be deemed a cold and mercenary calculation;
but we must say, that instead of attempting an amalgamation
of the two races—Europeans and Zealanders,—as is*

*recommended by some persons, the wiser course
would be, to let the native race gradually retire
before the settlers, and ultimately become extinct."*

The colonists, alas,
did not always pipe to this plan:
Come live with me and be my love. . . .

*Under the bam, under the boo,
two live as one, one live as two,
under the bamboo tree. . . .*

*

Down the beach from Plymouth,
where my wife's ancestors once landed,
the tide creeps in. Gulls

squawk and soar. Back sprawled
on the hot sands, a napping
brown-skinned girl. And up the hill

a young white hunter
volleyballer stares unabashedly
as only the young, white, and restless can.

This soap opera sings my life,
and like the colonial tales
will end in death and desire

and that strange urgent beast
hybridity. Or,
more simply, my daughter,

the necessary *happa* needle in my heart.

The Last Days

An ordinary day
in early autumn, last tomatoes
and sunflowers lifting
their stalks to the light,
and the heat still hovering
as if August never ends,
though it already has.
From the bushes the Buddha
steps forth, like those ballplayers
in *The Field of Dreams*,
a corny movie even for
Iowa and Kevin Costner,
but such is my vision,
and though he looks nothing
like Keanu Reeves, and could
be any slender Oriental
in a flowing orange robe
like those monks who pyred
their way, for a nanosecond,
into the American psyche,
somehow I know
it's him because he is
the Buddha, after all.
He says, "You possess now
seventy-six days more,
what will you write of
your life?" I stare into eyes
wrinkled with a smile as
a monarch with sore feet
floats down on his shoulders
and the crows on the wires
have all flown off, and I
ask, "Why November 12th?"
since I'm Asian and good

with numbers, and he says,
"13 is a cliché, though not
really in the Indian calendar."
In the whirlwind that ensues,
I think of Samantha first,
my silent and sullen
fourteen-year-old daughter
who will call her mother
bitch in the next few months
just to set herself free
to make love to the world
in her own fierce way;
and then of Nikko
who cannot be yelled at
or he'll burst into tears
and yet I yell anyway
knowing this is the way
the world answers back
as I was so much like him,
crawling as a boy
beneath the stairs to bawl
and curl to a fetal crouch
at the words of Michael Ogata
"You big fat ape." And now
it's Tomo, our oldest soul,
who, when the man stood
on the Franklin Avenue Bridge,
later admonished his mother
she should have unloosened
her grip, let him talk the man
down from his urge to fly
for flying is only for birds
and the butterflies, and she
stared and knew he was right.
And I think of her without whom
these wouldn't exist
and the years of my unfaithfulness,
and the years I pushed away

whiteness and sometimes her,
and how I pushed away this voice
as if it were a curse or a gift
rejected, bitter as Timon
wanting to feed to my enemies
pieces of their children and she
so bewildered and fearing,
like so many of her tribe,
that darkness inside me
and wanting it shut tight
in a closet and not loose
and wandering the rooms
of our house late at night
or greeting our children
at breakfast each morning.
But that is all over, now,
thank the Buddha,
and so I ask him no more
questions, for I know,
as he steps back into
the bushes where lilacs will
blossom without me next
spring, I will write of them
for the rest of my days
and this will be all
I will leave on this earth.

For Years

The artist's daughter did not notice
the years missing
from the paintings he left her

like the corpses of tiny birds
lined up on a lawn
waiting for burial

or perhaps the devouring maw
of the neighborhood
tomcat. He

possessed such tiny hands,
she remembers,
and the puppet show

on her fourth birthday
where the three pigs
came on as a dog, a donkey,

and a panda, each
wondering about their
roles, confused by words

of a plot mastered
for someone else: Where
does such playing end

and death begin?
Or is the child not a daughter
when she remembers

his hand on her head
patting her thick black hair
as if implanting her beside

him when all she wanted
was to walk free
of his shadow, much warmer

in that sun? In childhood
we hibernate
in a wolf's belly

and are purged
as dung for the fields
where the first seedlings

emerge, stalking
the air with unfurling
and leafy shouts of joy

or sorrow or of both.
But the missing
years, where did they go?

In little graves in the garden?
In the blank snow of the canvas?
In his fist trembling

so from stroke, he could
no longer hold the brush,
dropping it with one

last splatter of black
ink on white, and night
beckoning outside

like a woman holding out
her arms, each ending
in two stunted stumps?

That is what the muse is:
Some years the child
disappears

from the family
and the family lives on
with its gossip

when truly it is the father
who has left all
this undone. So

she picks up
the brush—hers, not his—
and paints a tiny

bird corpse
and a pain in her belly
says it will go on and on.

✤ IV ✤

On the Death & Life of the Yellow Poet Daredevil at the Franklin Ave. Bridge

No one spies behind your mask
the watery colors of
your face, spilling in the rain

down the gutters, festering
through sewers, rushing
a thousand miles downriver

to the Louisiana delta.
So you make your stand
at the bridge's edge

above the Mississippi,
a blind blues singer
with superhuman powers

in your ear, only the
rain blurs the outlines
of the cars whizzing past,

blast after blast
echoing gunshots in
your mind. As you hear

in the distance
a temple bell, monks
chant a sutra of pyres

risen from the stars
and light a body
at a Saigon intersection,

firing for the Buddha,
his breath bleating tongues
of glass: Peace, peace,

fades in the photographs
like the heroes of your skin
you never heard their tales. . . .

And everyone knows your motives
are wrong, as is
the acetylene suit you gather

to your body, leaping
the edge. How your yellow
skin burns as you hit

the surface, shattering to
a thousand pieces of song. . . .
(Only the black bobbing

head then emerges,
like Mao from the roiling
and more ancient Yangtze.)

Dahmer and the Boy

1. *A Traditional Life*

I dreamt of living beneath vast porticoes
where the sun sets the sea surface with fires
and cool white pillars frame the scene in rows
and basalt shadows cave over darker desires.

There waves roll in a water-mirrored sky,
and turbulent oceanic solemnities
cast a music so rich, a mystical sigh
sings down the sun in the sea's declivities.

So I sank in that voluptuous calm,
a milieu of azure, so vague and splendid,
and the perfume of naked slaves attended

as they fanned my brow with waving palms:
Slaves whose sole concern was to uncover
what dolorous secret saddened their master.

2. *Preliminary Interviews*

Would you like a drink?

No. No thank you. [Smile.] I've already eaten.

Can you talk about what happened?

What? Oh. I suppose so.

When do you believe it started?

Probably in Ohio. Long ago.

In childhood?

It was quite ordinary. If that's what you're asking.

Did you have any friends?

Not really. I didn't fit in. Or so they said.

Were you close to your mother?

She didn't live with us.

And your father?

I don't know. I don't think it was anything in his control.

So how did it start?

Somehow it just happened. I can't really say how. . . .

*

To anatomize and preserve as a boy
their small-boned bodies,

I splayed them out on a cutting board, wings,
claws, fur and feathers, whiskers

and teeth, beaks
for crying out

as babies
in the nest, asking their sufferance

of worms, of caterpillars and beetles, ladybugs
on which

they lived as infants, and lived on as adults:
I pickled them

in a magical
brine, echoed a process ancient

as Egypt, cradle
of civilizations. There is a secret

I believe, an elixir over death
like the medieval relics of clerics

in dank cloisters, fostering a cult
of bodies and their parts, hair, teeth, nails

clipped from eternity, for eternity.
Last week

the priest asked if I thought I possessed
a soul. I

stared at him for several seconds: Who
was he

to talk of the soul? What has
he devoured

except a wafer
which he takes for flesh

even a child
knows isn't flesh

but flour, egg and water
baked in an oven

like bread, like common bread?

*

In the last five years, the United States, with only five per cent of the world's population, has produced seventy percent of the world's serial killers.

Jeffrey Dahmer: Born, 1960. White male. 17 male victims, mostly black and Hispanic. Two Asians.

As for the science of taxidermy, hunters like to keep trophies.

(The local Legion with its deers' heads on the walls.)

A brass bowl of fruit. Incense. Before the gods.

Dahmer built a small shrine of human heads, limbs, genitals.

Problem: How to make the flesh numen.

3. *A Laotian Song*

Fourteen year-old Konerak Sinthasomphone was found by the police running naked and in handcuffs in the street outside Dahmer's apartment: "The intoxicated Asian naked male [laughter in the background] was returned to sober boyfriend and we're ten-eight. . . ."
(Police transcript)

*

Here is all I think I will recall of earth—

Sprinkle sprigs of coriander and mint,
translucent noodles, squid and shrimp
curling in fatted broth, laced with lime;

now drop red iridescence of pepper oil
so pungent sweat pops from your brow,
beads that glisten on the grass just before dawn:

I can still see my birdlike mother at the stove,
her fist, gnarled and weathered with spots, stirring
with a wooden spoon her ancient black pot.

She's singing a song she learned as a girl
as she carried a basket of laundry on her head,
walking other maidens to the river in Vientiane.

I don't know if she was ever beautiful,
but I like to see her that way, so young
and hair so black the light sinks inside it.

One morning a strange boy approached her.
She looked up and saw in his smile a gold
capped tooth: That, she said, was your father.

She told me so little of Laos, the old country.
Water buffalo in rice paddies, palm-lined roads.
The sultry gardens of the capital city.

All she would say was that there was this war.
People started to die. More and more.
Until she knew it was no longer her home.

(My father? He was one of those who died.)
Better, she said, to drink up your soup, son.
Better to learn English. This American tongue.

4. Prayers

Who has not, in nightmare,

suddenly seized

an image so despicable, so horrifying, so sick, almost
always it vanishes

the moment
you wake, scarcely

a glint remaining—
                              a fist or knife.
a sexual tongue penetrating
parent or child or other holy figure—

and the ditch foaming
with blood or shit or sperm

suddenly vanishes,

and you're whole, alive and moral once more,
and not

the depraved being whose imagination fostered those images
ancient and barbaric and beyond

recall. And yet

there are some, like me, who see those images—
it was no dream, I lay broad waking—

even after the nightmare
ends. . . . Yes. I saw someone's heart

in a dish; it sat steaming before me,
I sliced it open

and there lay all the ventricles
of my life, the meal

I so desired—Who placed that vision

inside me? Could I
have chosen it?

And if I had,
        would that make me
                                more
or less
        insane?

        *

As for the missing—

No posters on milk cartons.
No rewards. No ten o'clock bulletins.
They perished as the wind,
trash scattering city streets,
vacant lots and blind alleys.
Where emptiness had been.

You'd think they'd flee from me,
Massa, bwanna, boss-san.
But locked inside each beauty
bounds the beast snarling to be
free—What we desire most
is always the forbidden.

Flesh so dark I pursued,
succulent erotic fruit,
mango, pomegranate,
an eggplant's iridescent shine,
muscular meaty walnut,
so salty, sweet, and ripe:

I don't recall exactly when
I caught that first strange perfume
of what sizzled in the pan;
how urgently aromas
lingered after, wafting from
my kitchen to my bedroom.

Lathering after in the shower,
I steamed and scoured my skin;
slipped naked in the sheets,
and prayed for my own end.
Prayed I'd be able to sleep,
it would not happen again.

—The Lord granted none of these.

Neuromancer *Poetics*

> *Someone must have been telling lies about Joseph*
> *K., for without having done anything wrong he*
> *was arrested one fine morning.*
> —Franz Kafka, *The Trial*

. . . In a cyber-blue world there appears an atoll.
I'm drifting on a rusted-out hull,
my skin darker than its sides, but unburnt.
Once atomic blasts left only the roaches.

Have I come to the end of my searches?
Our apocalypse leaves me these sharks
whose fins swirl about me,
marks on a screen of electric memory:

The illusion is the illusion's not real.
An alien touches his image on the glassy
surface, and this is what he feels—
The modem connects with a harsh rasping.

Call me sometime, said the past.
(By the way, the number's unlisted.)

*

But who returns now to that darkened planet
which hurled white moons above us, half eaten,
our face a mess of shadows and unwanted
as sands where we slept as deserted creatures?

Once our whole family boarded an astral bus.
They're coming for us, said sister.
Which translated with the last master
to: They're coming out of us.

What was it about our features
which so frightened them?
Something in our eyes, our skin's odd tincture.
Did we take their virus into that prison

or find it simmering in our bloodstream
the moment we absorbed their moon's blank beam?

*

Seeing how aliens had already landed.
Seeing how the dead defiled the living.
Who replicated quickly as vermin did,
then doubled in our sight without a warning.

Now they walked the streets among us
as if no one suspected in broad daylight
how brazenly they could ignore our disgust,
how brilliantly they bought our disguises.

How the old android spun inward, unable to speak,
over and over, like a dervish.
As if a hologram of hands and feet
might imitate the itch of flesh to perish.

(The war of the worlds did not quite occur this way.
Though none of us recalls the program or the exact day.)

*

Mr. K. meet Mr. Dahmer.
He's into deepfreeze as preservation.
Unlike you he's a charmer.
Keeps his lovers close to the gut.

Friday night on the Nikkei.
No *sarareemen*, just hopped up *gaijin*.
Haze like a burnt-out television screen.
By the mercurial waters of Tokyo Bay.

The snitch told K. the WRA wanted him dead
for delaying the transfer of a synthetic
glandular extract with margins so wide
they just might claw their way back.

Now Dahmer's the one with the connections
K. with wires so fried you can smell the carbon.

*

For the secret Asian man the agent is yellow,
a cat-and-mouse game in a neural corridor
where each door opens as before,
but never the same since after the war.

Neither suave nor unhandsome but electrically charged,
code numbers as bumpers for hitting hard:
Crash some asshole who slows down before you,
won't let you zoom the information highway—

Such diction lacks some oxygen,
possesses a twentieth-century feel.
Idoru counts X's and O's in the new millennium.
The shift into hyperspace ain't a fiction:

I'm waiting for you Keiko, K. types.
But it's *yoru* now and not tonight.

✤ V ✤

Hyde Park, 1950

Near the gym door my father lounges
with his pal Mas at an all Nisei dance.
A grad student at U.C., he should be
scrawling in the margins of *The Tempest*,

but there's other matter now to digest—
Such as this Nisei princess,
gabbing with her cohorts across the floor,
bobby-soxers in saddle shoes and pleated skirts.

She holds a cup of punch in her hand,
and laughter tumbles from her face so aquiline
and sure, with a nose of Utamaro's beauties
though her hair's curled and pure Patti Page.

As he stares at this all-American vision,
he does not think of his father's nursery
as she does not recall the green grocery
in Seattle, all her father's life labors lost.

They're a new generation, postwar, free.
Still he knows they share some history.
For seconds after he's spied her, he turns,
grabs the lapel of Mas's secondhand suit,

and shouts above the strains of Tommy Dorsey,
"That's the girl. That's the girl I'm going to marry."
Then struts across the half court and foul line
and just beneath the basket she looks up,

finds this figure so strapping for a Nisei,
with hair slicked back, face both rounded and lean,
almost, I'll see years after in the photos,
a *Nihon* version of the young Muhammad Ali.

Oh moment of their—and my—beginning,
which years later, when I asked for her version,
she looked at me sharply, "Oh David, why?"
How it floats like a butterfly, stings like a bee.

Internment Epistles

Dear Hanaye,

A cold snap blew in today, stinging
our faces as we trudged to mess,
rifling my coat like a guard.

The slop they serve sickens me.
Why eat? (And yet I know, I know:
At this same moment millions starve.)

Frost whitens the windowpane
with intricate leafy designs,
and I conjure there rows of tomatoes

or strawberries, blossoms of color
as I travel in my mind backwards
to the fields we harvested

together, you so young and shy
still, a beautiful beautiful bride
who braved an ocean for this harsh

and lush land and the raw callused
hands of a farmer who dreamed
of *Bon O-dori* celebrations, his sons

pounding *taiko*, daughters
dancing *buyo*, chrysanthemums
bursting from rippling kimonos:

Why did you come? Why did I stay?
Such thoughts slip like icy winds
through the cracks, and I cannot

hold them back. And yet,
in a Mason jar on my desk,
swims a baby whitefish

by a sprig of snapdragon,
saved from the fall, as if I
still owned a glorious garden.

Take these coal-black characters,
Hanaye, take them as footsteps
across a frozen white tundra

and know that as the salmon
spears against the cold current,
I am forever flailing toward you. . . .

My dear husband,

Received two letters and one postcard.
I cannot apologize enough for my silence.

Fever and coughing keep me up at night,
yet my dreams are worse than illness,
unsettling images of fire, temples

and houses crushed like a boy's kite
and ants scurrying out from hissing flames:
Last night one possessed my mother's face.

She held out her hands, each palm a pyre,
and asked me to drink and be saved.
Father Fukuda says pay these no mind;

he begs me to pray to his Jesus,
nailed to a post, a beast on a gibbet,
as if torture required tortuous belief.

I try to think of the bodhisattva shade
where Buddha sat, a hissing cobra
at his back, contemplating No-Mind:

His cobra slithered away. Mine does not.
(Like these barracks my thoughts overflow,
couples arguing, babies bawling, love sounds at night. . . .)

Christmas was lonely. I cried and cried.
George at training camp, Kimiko at college.
You in that prison they won't call a prison.

Me, a bird in a cage, who's stopped her singing. . . .
They have given me a single room now.
For my nerves. For my nerves I knit,

but sometimes as I pearl and stitch,
the yarn tangles and I forget
for whom I web this scarf.

I tell myself it is you.
But when I try to bring back your face,
that is when my No-Mind appears.

Forgive me, dear husband.
I shouldn't be telling you all this.
I will try to write more next time.

I will try to heal. . . .

Dear Hanaye,

Waiting anxiously to receive your reply
to the important matters in my letter
of December 7. *(How that date*

now chimes inside me: pounding at
the door, the men in their dark raincoats
striding like bandits into our living room,

yanking open my desk, the dressers,
rummaging our closets, letters
I sent you after our omiyai;

the plaque from the Japanese
literary society proclaiming
my triumph in haiku

and the map Kimiko scrawled
for a high-school assignment
of the Panama canal—

all that incriminated us
in their eyes: Not one of them
thought to take off his hat.)

I received the chocolates you sent,
so I assume you must be okay.
Perhaps my letter has gone astray.

My appeal and other documents
to file with the Attorney General
are ready, but without a word

from you, I'm at a loss.
Perhaps you are ill,
I think, and my mind goes wild

with images I sever
to prevent following
where they may lead.

I tell myself it must be Christmas
and preparations for *Bon O-dori*
that keeps you busy, as this

last day of the year it rains:
I am carving a model boat,
a tiny anchor of sandstone.

Hanaye, let us sail away
from all this, and anchor
our craft in Haname bay. . . .

My dear husband,

I received your letter yesterday.
A thousand apologies. Please
do not read into my silence.
Yes, I've been ill. But now

I am gaining weight. I force
myself to the *magusa* they serve
and though sometimes I feel
like a pig at a trough, I chew

and swallow and think of slices
of *maguro* and *hamachi*,
unagi unrolled across a bed
of rice, golden sliced orbs

of *tsukemono*, like tiny suns:
And my belly grows warmer
as if another child grew
there, as we so often wished.

Dr. Mitsumori, Ishibashi,
even the Pastor have helped me so.
And your lovely model ship.
Surely you are my anchor.

I do suffer some insomnia.
Perhaps it's simply old age.
I don't need my dreams anymore.
I know what they amount to.

Uncle Koike still acts strangely.
I try to talk to him though.
He keeps losing his money.
He tells me it's the gambling

and sake, so drunk on the way
home, someone beat
and robbed him of everything
he owned. I laugh and tell him:

Ojii-chan, it was just a dream.
It was just a dream. . . .
He looks at me as if I'm
the crazy one. *Bakkatare,*

he mutters. But I know
he doesn't mean it.
Yesterday, though, he tried
to kiss me, calling me Sachiko,

and I kept telling him Sachiko's
dead, Sachiko's dead. He
let go of me and stared
at his hands, and with his left

traced the lifeline of his right
as if searching for where
she went. He began weeping
then, into his cupped palms. . . .

Iwao, my hands are shaking.
I can't write any longer.
I thank Buddha for my blessings,
what strength I still possess.

Dear Hanaye,

Tadao-san wove this cigarette case
from the strands of a potato sack.
I rolled the cigarettes myself.

I will think of you sitting
on the barracks steps, smoking:
Blow, for me, a few smoke rings.

We'll communicate like the Indians
from a great distance,
and I'll know you're all right.

My rehearing's next week.
I try not to think about it.
I'm almost as restless

as when Yukio—I mean George—
was born (isn't it strange
how so many sons assume this name

as if they too could give birth
to this country. Better
to borrow the name Geronimo,

who refused his prison
and vanished in mountains
where none could find him.)

In the shallows of the river
near camp, Tadao and I
dug up clams and kelp.

We roasted the clams
on a tin drum and pickled
the kelp into *tsukudani*

and ate them with mushrooms
we found by the willows:
their texture, earthy and dark,

reminded me of my hands
and how they must have smelled
to you, and I found both shame

and delight in that.
Tadao-san laughed we were a pair
of *ronin*, growing fat

off the land. Not fat,
I said, but skinny, skinny
as two scavenging crows,

and for a moment
as the juice of the clams
dribbled down our chins

I forget where we are.
It will get colder soon.
Another season passes

and we are still apart.
Please be more careful now.
I can't but feel it's almost done.

My dear husband,

Thank you for the dried salmon.
And the candy and the "Jimminy Cricket."
The salmon was salty and pungent and tough.

I devoured it like a woman, alone and starving.
You know, one of those witches in Noh,
with her hut deep in the forest, who foresees

all that has passed, all that will come,
and traps journeyers with her beauty
and elegant dance and delicate kimono.

But when the night falls
and she unchignons her hair
and the silk cloth drops at her feet,

no flesh steps forth, just glittering scales
and a serpent's hiss, the tongue seeking
a companion for punishment and eternity—

I'm afraid sometimes that trapped traveler
is you. Such a gentle and simple pilgrim,
a woodsman who's labored years

for a pittance, and yet, will not give up
his cutting and hauling, though all he gathers
the flames devour, transmogrifying

to black black ash. So I pray for green
sagebrush to cover the white mountains
which stand before me like sentinels

that bar the way and trap me
with these days that pass shamelessly
as my eyes flutter and blink

and cannot believe what they see
and so believe what surfaces at night
when they are closed and witches dream.

Perhaps this is merely age. Or nerves.
Or simply an old lady's unsettling moods.
I pray for your health. I'll write when I'm better. . . .

Dear Hanaye,

I have just received the telegram.
I ripped the star from the window.
Wept from a place inside I did not know.

But when I stopped—but it has not stopped—
I picked up the crumpled cloth strip,
smoothed it out and hung it up again.

Once I believed in the weaver girl
and the herd boy who, torn
apart in their constellations

up in the black black sky, once yearly,
across the spaces of the universe
and the River of Heaven,

came together and held each
other's hand, so briefly
it must have mattered.

Now, Hanaye, you must not let go.
There is a new star there.
It will not fall again. . . .

Dear Hanaye,

It's bitter cold. Minus sixteen.
In these rickety barracks
my breath forms frozen clouds

as if my lungs only gave out ghosts.
There's the smell of leftover
Kikkoman in my tiny room

as if a feast had just been devoured
and the partyers vanished
and the silence is fuller

for the echoes it holds.
How have you been feeling
lately? I tell myself you're better.

And for once I don't know
whether it is or is not a lie.
As I told you before

it won't be long before the sun
shines upon us both
as it did that day I took your hand

at Tokyo Bay and pointed east
and across the silver scales
of sea glittering in the sun,

mirroring our glorious future,
our home, and our children lay.
So far away that time,

our flesh so close I could sense
your breathing and matched it
with mine and my imaginings.

Beneath the far peaks
snowy fields wait like a blank page
for me to write one last message:

No wonder you slipped.
It's a sea of ice, you know.
Sparkling in sunlight.

You should have warned me.
Old woman of white,
you have to be alive to tell the tale. . . .

A Winter's Tale

How did I lose and find my life?
The stars have their homes,
the moon needs no country,
and the snow
distilling
its icy existence
to a moment on my palm
fears no vanishing
but falls
and falls in its dreaming
and real existence. So
I stand in my yard
staring up at the window
where your face
might appear, calling me
in, bathed in the sweat
of my running mile
after mile up the river
in search of the body
that leaves me
no wisdom
but only the soft
flaking and fattening
of a soul past forty.
If I were a young
lover, I would fly
like a sprite
up to that window, scraping
to be let in, calling
your name like a wound
in my side, and only
your touch like a preacher
electrified with the godhead
lightning the believer, fainting

him back to earth,
might conjure a salve
to the slashing
you've left me to hold.
But I'm no longer
twenty, I'm only scooping
snow from the walk, not
bleeding in the cold. And that
same sweet light up there
stays me these moments
where your face won't
appear, as you know
already what I'll do
moments from now—
Open the door and walk
as I have half my life
back into yours.

Notes

"Relocations": *Bakka*—idiot, dummy.

"No Epic Song": *gohan*—rice (also meal). *hana fuda*—Japanese card game. *ojii-san*—Grandfather. *biwa*—Japanese stringed instrument. Minidoka— Minidoka internment camp. *hashi*—chopstick.

"Bruyères (1944)": *Okaa-san*—mother. *hayaku*—hurry.

"First Generation Angels": *pho*—Vietnamese soup.

"Black Angels: Latasha Harlins": In the tape from the store's video monitor, it's clear that Latasha Harlins had already turned and was walking away from the counter when she was shot by the store clerk, Sun Ja Du. Du was found guilty of voluntary manslaughter and sentenced to five years probation, four hundred hours of community service, and a five-hundred-dollar fine. The sentencing occurred five months before the jury in the Rodney King trial returned not-guilty verdicts on all charges, except one count of excessive force against one officer (a mistrial was declared on that count).

"Minneapolis Public": *happa*—a mixed race person.

"Legend": Abercrombie & Fitch set off protests by the Asian-American community with the production of t-shirts using racial stereotypes (one depicted two slant-eyed men in conical hats and the slogan "Wong Brothers Laundry Service—Two Wongs Can Make It White"). Awhile later, *Sixty Minutes* did a segment on the company's hiring practices, where employees maintained that they were discouraged by the company from hiring people of color or advised to place employees of color in the stock room.

"*Neuromancer* Poetics": *gaijin*—foreigners. WRA—Wartime Relocation Authority. Nikkei—Japanese who settled in American (or abroad) are sometimes referred to as *Nikkeijin* (though there's also a pun here on the Japanese stock exchange as well as a salute to the Ninsei, site of the opening scene of William Gibson's *Neuromancer*). *Idoru*—heroine of William Gibson's novel of the same name and the Japanese pronounciation of "idol." *yoru*—night (though this is also how the Japanese might pronounce "your").

"Hyde Park, 1950": *Nihon*—Japanese.

"Internment Epistles": *taiko*—Japanese drum. *buyo*—Japanese dance. *Omiyai*—the meeting portion of an arranged marriage. *magusa*—fodder. Though the poem is a fiction, it uses a few phrases from the letters of Iwao and Hanaye Matsushita in *Imprisoned Apart: The World War II Correspondence of an Issei Couple*, edited by Louis Fiset (University of Washington Press).

Acknowledgments

Asian-Pacific American Journal: "The Young Asian Women";

Cafe Solo: "Bruyères (1944)";

Hamline Review: "Astronomy";

Journal of the Asian American Renaissance: "Suite for *Miss Saigon*," "Years Later";

Pequod: "Dahmer and the Boy" (from section 3 & 4);

Poetry International: "No Epic Song" (sections 1, 3)

"Island Angel" appeared in *American Voices, American Visions* (Harry N. Abrahms, Inc., 2000).

"Words on My Tongue" and "Father Blues for Jon Jang" first appeared in *Another Way to Dance: Contemporary Voices of Asian-American/Asian-Canadian Poetry* (TSAR Publications).

"Relocations" first appeared in *Breaking Silence: An Anthology of Contemporary Asian-American Poets* (The Greenfield Review Press, 1981).

"A Winter's Tale" first appeared in *Good Company* (Grinnell College, 2000).

"In the Video Store at Chicago & Lake" first appeared in *Manthology: Poems of The Male Experience* (Invisible Cities Press, 2002).

The prose section in "Suite for *Miss Saigon*" originally appeared in an article in *Mother Jones*.

Sections of "Dahmer and the Boy" and "First Generation Angels" first appeared in *Poems of the New Century* (David R. Godine, 2002).

"Minneapolis Public" first appeared in *These United States: Original Essays by Leading American Writers on Their State within the Union,* ed. by John Leonard (Thunder Mouth's Press/Nation Books, 2003).

My thanks to the publications and editors in which the above poems appeared, sometimes in an earlier version. I want to thank Garrett Hongo, Alexs Pate, Traise Yamamoto, Marilyn Chin, Junot Diaz, Li-Young Lee, Jay White, Diem Jones, Veena Deo, Quincy Troupe, Thom Ward, Elmaz Abinader, Wakako Yamauchi, and the late Esther Suzuki for their support and encouragement. My appreciation to Long Nguyen for his brilliant cover art. And a special thanks, as always, to my wife Susan Sencer.

"Words on My Tongue" is for Li-Young Lee.
"Internment Epistles" is for Garrett Hongo.

About the Author

David Mura is a poet, creative nonfiction writer, critic, playwright, and performance artist. His second book of poetry, *The Colors of Desire* (Anchor-Random, 1995), won the Carl Sandburg Literary Award from the Friends of the Chicago Public Library. His first, *After We Lost Our Way* (Carnegie Mellon U. Press), won the 1989 National Poetry Series Contest.

Mura has written two memoirs: *Turning Japanese: Memoirs of a Sansei* (Anchor-Random), which won a 1991 Josephine Miles Book Award from the Oakland PEN and was listed in the New York Times Notable Books of Year, and *Where the Body Meets Memory: An Odyssey of Race, Sexuality and Identity* (Anchor-Random, 1996). His book of critical essays, *Song for Uncle Tom, Tonto & Mr. Moto: Poetry & Identity*, appeared in the U. of Michigan Press Poets on Poetry series (2002). Along with novelist Alexs Pate, Mura has created and performs a multimedia performance piece, *Secret Colors*, about their lives as men of color and Asian-American/African-American relations. A film adaptation of this piece, *Slowly, This*, was broadcast in the PBS series *ALIVE TV*.

Mura has served as the Artistic Director of the Asian American Renaissance and has taught at the Voices of the Nation Association, Hamline University, University of Minnesota, St. Olaf College, the Loft, and the University of Oregon. Among his awards are a Lila Wallace *Reader's Digest* Writers' Award, a US/Japan Creative Artist Exchange Fellowship, NEA Fellowships, Bush Fellowships, and Loft-McKnight Writers' Awards. He gives readings and speaks on the issues of race and diversity throughout the country. He lives in Minneapolis with his wife, Dr. Susan Sencer, and three children, Samantha, Nikko, and Tomo.

BOA EDITIONS, LTD.: AMERICAN POETS CONTINUUM SERIES

❧ *Colophon* ❧

Angels for the Burning by David Mura
was set in Abobe Garamond with Woodtype Ornaments
by Richard Foerster, York Beach, Maine.
The cover was designed by Daniel Wanglin, Drexel Hill, Pennsylvania.
The cover art, "Homage to Boat People" by Long Nguyen
is courtesy of the artist.
Manufacturing was by McNaughton & Gunn, Lithographers,
Ann Arbor, Michigan.

The publication of this book was made possible, in part, by the special
support of the following individuals:

Alan & Nancy Cameros
Dr. & Mrs. Gary H. Conners
Suzanne & Peter Durant
Dr. Henry & Beverly French
Judy & Dane Gordon
Gerard & Suzanne Gouvernet
Kip & Deb Hale
Peter & Robin Hursh
Robert & Willy Hursh
Archie & Pat Kutz
Rosemary & Lew Lloyd
Boo Poulin
Deborah Ronnen
Robert Shea
Bruce & Madeleine Sweet
Pat & Michael Wilder